USING A WHEELCHAIR

BY
ROBIN TWIDDY

KidHaven
PUBLISHING

A DIFFERENT WORLD

Published in 2022 by
KidHaven Publishing, an Imprint of Greenhaven Publishing, LLC
353 3rd Avenue
Suite 255
New York, NY 10010

Edited by: John Wood
Designed by: Gareth Liddington

Cataloging-in-Publication Data

Names: Twiddy, Robin.
Title: Using a wheelchair / Robin Twiddy.
Description: New York : KidHaven Publishing, 2022. | Series: A different world | Includes glossary and index.
Identifiers: ISBN 9781534538481 (pbk.) | ISBN 9781534538504 (library bound) | ISBN 9781534538498 (6 pack) | ISBN 9781534538511 (ebook)
Subjects: LCSH: Children with disabilities--Juvenile literature. | Paraplegics--Juvenile literature. | Wheelchairs--Juvenile literature.
Classification: LCC HV903.T95 2022 | DDC 305.9'08083--dc23

Printed in the United States of America

CPSIA compliance information: Batch #CSKH22: For further information contact Greenhaven Publishing LLC, New York, New York at 1-844-317-7404.

Please visit our website, www.greenhavenpublishing.com. For a free color catalog of all our high-quality books, call toll free 1-844-317-7404 or fax 1-844-317-7405.

This book was written and designed with accessibility for people with color vision deficiency and dyslexia in mind.

Photo credits:

Cover & Throughout – CkyBe, Serhii Bobyk, Evgenii Emelianov, Rvector, Mark Rademaker, SunshineVector, iamtui7, 2 – ESB Professional, 4&5 – wavebreakmedia, AnnGaysorn, 6&7 – wavebreakmedia, Jaren Jai Wicklund, CGN089, 8&9 – xiaorui, Jevgeni Mironov, jax10289, 10&11 – New Africa, Edvard Nalbantjan, Photographee.eu, A-photographyy, 12&13 – Monkey Business Images, Andrey_Popov, 14&15 – Toa55, Goldsithney, 16&17 – Helen Hotson, 18&19 – ACHPF, A.RICARDO, 20&21 – ALPA PROD, Alla Greeg, 22&23 – ChiccoDodiFC, wavebreakmedia.

All facts, statistics, web addresses, and URLs in this book were verified as valid and accurate at time of writing.
No responsibility for any changes to external websites or references can be accepted by either the author or publisher.

CONTENTS

Words that look like <u>this</u> can be found in the glossary on page 24.

A DiFFERENT WORLD?

We all live in the same world, don't we? Well, for some people the world can seem a little different. People who use wheelchairs face <u>challenges</u> in places that others might not.

In this book you will have the chance to see a little bit of what the world can be like for someone who uses a wheelchair. It is important to understand how others see the world and the challenges they face.

WHO USES A WHEELCHAIR?

Wheelchairs are mobility aids. This means that they help people to move around.

All sorts of people use wheelchairs. Even though these people are all different, they all use a wheelchair for the same reason: to help them get around.

Some people have used wheelchairs since they were very young, while others start using them later in life. Some people only use wheelchairs some of the time.

Many people use wheelchairs because of an injury. Other people may have illnesses that make it difficult or <u>impossible</u> to walk.

DIFFERENT WHEELCHAIRS

There are lots of different types of wheelchairs. The type that someone uses depends on what their needs are. Here are a few different types.

Electric wheelchair

Manual wheelchair

Electric wheelchair with <u>elevating mechanism</u>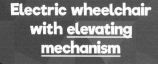

Choosing the right type of wheelchair can be very difficult. It is important to get the best one for the person's needs, especially if they are going to be spending a lot of time in it.

AT HOME

Bathroom

Stairs

Adeel and Mei go to the same school, but their homes are very different. This is what Mei's house looks like inside.

Adeel's house is a little different because he uses a wheelchair. Can you see some of the things that are different?

Bathroom

Stairlift

Adeel needs room for his wheelchair and for things to be in reach when he is in his wheelchair.

ACCESSIBILITY

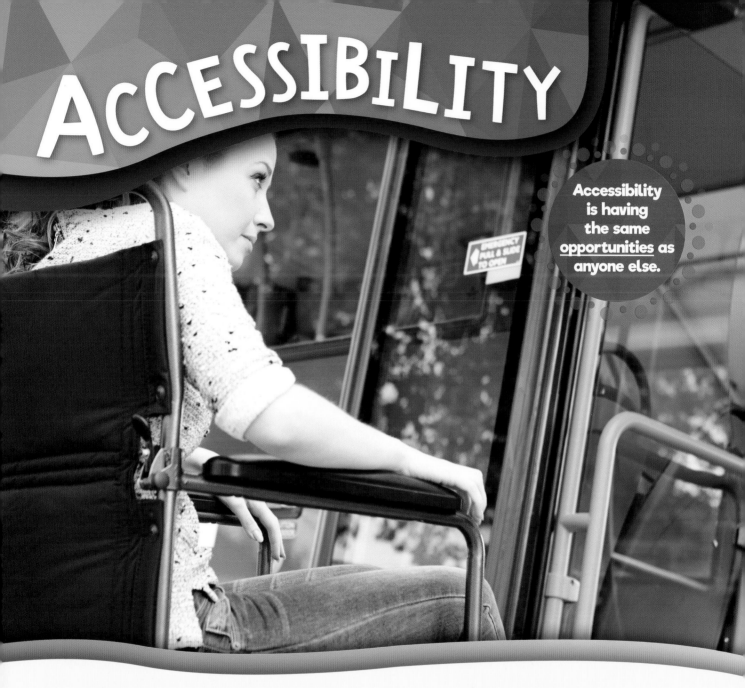

Accessibility is having the same opportunities as anyone else.

Accessibility means being able to use something without an <u>impairment</u> holding you back. For someone who uses a wheelchair, that might mean having a ramp instead of a step.

Accessibility can be about having enough room for a person using a wheelchair to move around. If the tables in a restaurant are too close together, someone using a wheelchair might not be able to move around.

This table is accessible because it has room for a wheelchair.

MAKING CHANGES

Adeel needed ramps instead of steps in his house.

When Adeel first started using a wheelchair, his family needed to make a lot of changes around their house to make it more accessible.

Adeel didn't just need to change things in his home. Many people who use wheelchairs also need special vans to hold their wheelchair.

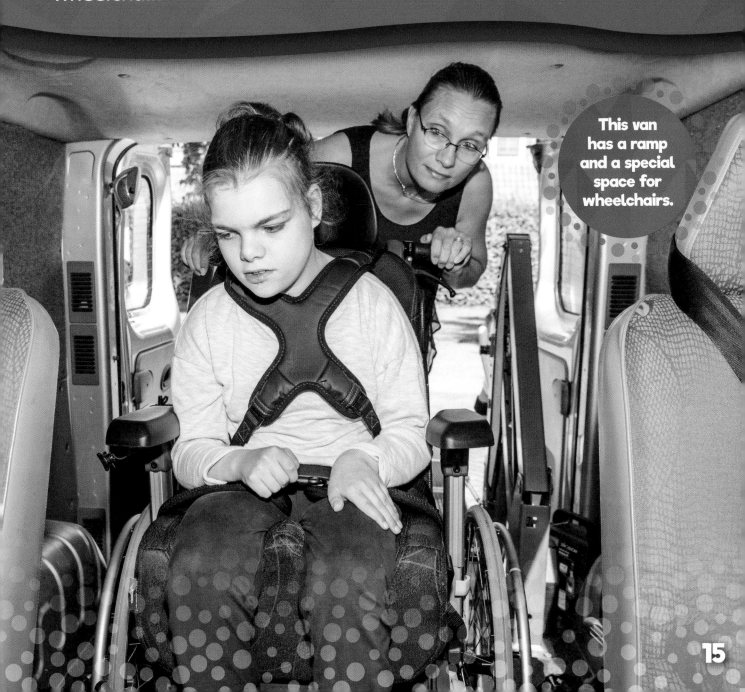

This van has a ramp and a special space for wheelchairs.

15

GOING SHOPPING

When Adeel and Mei go shopping, Mei doesn't have to think about how she is going to get into the stores.

People who use wheelchairs, like Adeel, have to think about all sorts of things. Does the store have a step? What kind of <u>surface</u> will the floor have? Will there be any steep hills?

Step

Hill

Cobbles

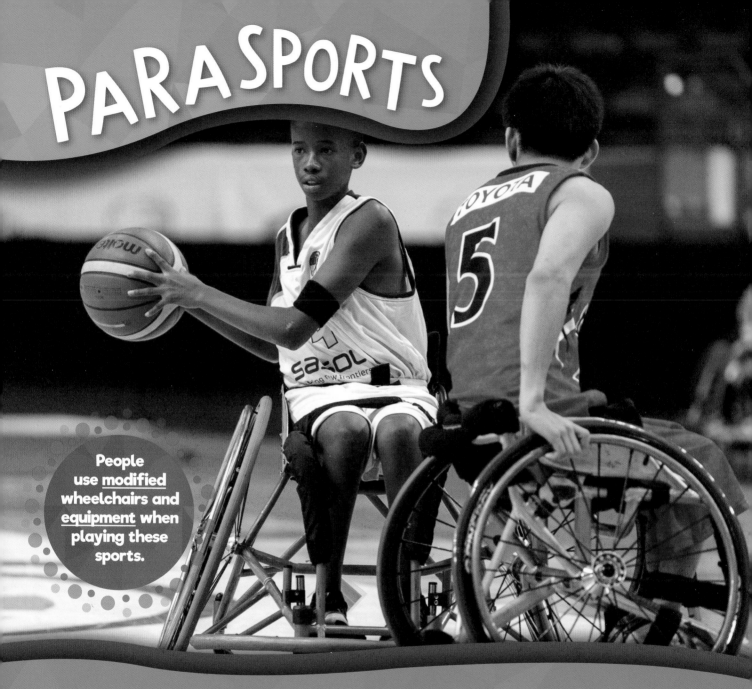

PARASPORTS

People use <u>modified</u> wheelchairs and <u>equipment</u> when playing these sports.

Parasports are played by people with impairments. Wheelchair basketball and wheelchair tennis are parasports that are played all over the world.

The Paralympic Games is a worldwide event where many parasports are played by some of the best athletes in the world. It is watched by millions of people on TV.

The 2016 Paralympic Games in Brazil

SuPPORT

Experts can help people make the right decisions.

There is a lot of support available for people who use wheelchairs. All people are different and have different needs. Wheelchairs and other support equipment can be expensive, but there are <u>charities</u> that can help.

Someone with a manual wheelchair might choose to wear special gloves when they use their wheelchair. This helps <u>protect</u> their hands and gives them more grip and control.

Manual wheelchairs move when the top of the wheel is pushed.

Going to the beach might be a challenge in a wheelchair. However, there is equipment that makes it easier to use a wheelchair on sand.

These wide steel wheels are good for moving across sand.

WE ARE ALL DIFFERENT

Even though people like Adeel may see the world a little differently, we are more alike, all of us, than we are different.

GLOSSARY

challenges	things that people must overcome to get or do what they want to
charities	organizations that try to help people and don't make any money
elevating mechanism	a machine that lifts or raises something
equipment	objects used for a special purpose
experts	people who are very knowledgeable about a topic
impairment	something that stops or holds a person back from doing something
impossible	cannot be done
modified	changed to work better in a different way
opportunities	chances to do or achieve something
protect	to stop or try to stop something from being harmed
surface	the top layer of a thing

INDEX

24